THE GREAT RIVER AND SMALL

Published for East Central State College, Ada, Oklahoma
by the UNIVERSITY OF OKLAHOMA PRESS : NORMAN

The Great River and Small and other poems

by WELBORN HOPE
Tramp Poet

INTRODUCTION BY *Guy Logsdon*

International Standard Book Number: 0–8061–0928–9

Library of Congress Catalog Card Number: 78–123344

Copyright 1970 by the University of Oklahoma Press, Publishing Division of the University. Composed and printed at Norman, Oklahoma, U.S.A., by the University of Oklahoma Press. First edition.

TO W. A. "*Gus*" *Delaney, Jr.*

Welborn Hope, Oklahoma's Tramp Poet, is one of those rare spirits who move freely through life, shunning the ambitions cherished by most of his fellow men—security, financial success, and those possessions that demonstrate success. In conventional terms Welborn is a self-determined failure. He has enjoyed his failure, however, far more profoundly than most individuals enjoy success and riches.

Welborn is highly successful in the two callings that he considers important—writing poetry and tramping. His poems, long recognized as the products of rare talent, have appeared in *Saturday Review*, *Poetry*, *The New Republic*, and newspapers across the country. Thirty-five years ago William Rose Benét, who published many of Welborn's poems in his *Saturday Review* column "The Phoenix Nest," wrote that a publisher would do well to sift through Welborn's poems for material for a book.

Throughout much of his adult life Welborn has been walking and thumbing his way around the country, convinced that, for the poet, stark ambition and the desire for material possessions are the poorest signs to follow on the road to self-fulfillment. Indeed, his great sorrow is that "society won't let a poet be as poor as he should be."

In Welborn's case the pressures of society were unavailing. He has been a tramp for thirty years. During the fifteen years before he permanently took to tramping the country, he periodically disappeared on short rambles, but awareness of his responsibility to his parents, who had no other children, always brought him home again.

"Home" was Ada, Oklahoma, where Thomas Welborn Hope was born on July 8, 1903, in what was then the Chickasaw Nation, Indian Territory. His father, Tom Hope, was Ada's first banker and, after 1911, the proprietor of one of the town's leading drugstores. Welborn's mother, Minnie Gazzelle Welborn Hope, was well educated for her time. She had earned a master's degree in education at Kidd Key College in Sherman, Texas, in 1891. In later years her activities in educational and civic causes earned her an entry in *Who's Who in America*. In fact, both of Welborn's parents were outstanding leaders in their pioneer southwestern community.

Welborn began writing poetry at an early age; his first published poem appeared in the *Ada Evening News* when he was seven years old. He was also scholastically precocious, graduating from East Central State College in Ada when he was eighteen years old. During Welborn's college years M. B. "Pop" Molloy, a professor of English, encouraged him to develop his poetic gifts. Welborn has always been grateful to Molloy for his teaching and inspiration.

Welborn's tramping desires were sparked in 1924, when he met and talked with Vachel Lindsay, the restless wanderer who in earlier years had traveled through the South and West, trading poems for bed and board. That meeting ultimately resulted in Welborn's decision to continue the traditions of tramp poets.

It was to be several years, however, before Welborn could fulfill his tramping desires. In 1930, to assist in the family business, he obtained a pharmacist's certificate—a feat that in those days required only a little experience and a fee of fifty dollars. For the next ten years he worked more or less regularly, wandering from home only when restlessness drove him.

Meanwhile, his nonconformist, individualistic ways were making him something of a controversial figure in his home town. In his scorn for the standard symbols of success he developed an almost evangelistic zeal to combat the world's material and spiritual hypocrisy. In his preoccupation with poetry he neglected the arts of the business world. He was truly happy only when he departed on a tramp—characteristically never by road but always across the open fields east of Ada.

In those travels he wandered throughout the Southwest, writing poems filled with the flavor and history of the region. Now and then he sent verses to Benét and to the editors of *Poetry*, who recognized his talent and published them. In 1940, after the deaths of his parents, having no marital attachments, he severed home ties and started on his lifelong tramp.

From the time he "hit the road," Welborn carried on the traditions of tramp poets, trading a poem for food, for shelter, for a ride—never taking without giving something in return. When necessary, he ate what the wilds of nature provided and slept under bridges, on sand bars, in fields or woods. For the most part his rides were with truck drivers and traveling salesmen needing a relief driver or craving companionship. When no ride was available, Welborn stopped to work until "ride times" were better. He has worked at almost every job imaginable, but only for the minimum necessities for survival. His friend Troy Gordon, a columnist for the *Tulsa World*, relates one occasion when he met Welborn on the street after a two-year interval and asked, "Welborn, are you working?" To which Welborn replied, "No, I worked last year."

His tramps have carried him across most of the nation. When asked about his most memorable tramp, he tells of walking from St. Louis to New Orleans—the tramp on which he wrote "The Great River and Small." Then he tells about being a self-invited guest in jail, paying a visit to Florida just before Pearl Harbor was attacked. He tells of picking cherries in Michigan, of cat-fishing on the Mississippi. He reminisces about his days in El Paso and Mexico and his adventures in the man-made canyons of New York City. It becomes obvious that all of his wanderings and all of his living constitute "one great tramp."

Now Welborn has reached an age that will not allow him to spend severe winters in the open. In the early spring of 1968, when asked why he had delayed starting his annual tramp, Welborn answered, "If you were up early this morning, you should know that this is not the most auspicious time to be taking a nap under a bridge." For the last few winters he has stayed in Tulsa, where friends and work await his return each fall. He has lived in various modest hotels and has often worked as clerk and switchboard operator in return for his room.

When spring comes, however, Welborn will again be on the road, a road he will follow as long as his health permits. His appearance will always be the same: he will be wearing slacks, a white shirt, a tie, a coat, and a weathered gray hat. His possessions will go with him, for all that he owns will fit into a small traveling bag. Wherever he goes, he will leave behind a poem—or a story, for he is a natural-born raconteur.

As a poet Welborn has successfully contrasted and related the "old" Southwest and the new, and he has given poetic, spiritual countenance to all the regions through which he has tramped. The poems about his native region spring from a thorough knowledge of its history and from insights gained in his wanderings that have preserved in him the burning spirit of the frontier. That spirit, combined with his compassionate, retrospective vision of life in the Southwest, has enabled him to create an expression of complex emotions, free of romanticism, that no other writer of the region, whether poet or historian, has been able to capture. His poems about other regions are unique expressions of his spiritual experience of them.

Welborn and my father, Guy Logsdon, were good friends in Ada. My cousin, Conner Logsdon, also a friend of Welborn's, saved manuscripts of poems that Welborn gave him when he left Ada. As a boy in Ada, I often heard my father, Conner, and others tell stories about the strange, almost legendary tramp poet who would periodically disappear from town and just as suddenly reappear. It became a great desire of mine to meet this man.

In the fall of 1967 I learned that Welborn was in Tulsa. After a few phone calls I found him at the Detroit Hotel. The visits that he and I have since exchanged have been the most enjoyable and enlightening conversations in my experience. It has been a privilege to come to know a man I consider to be one of the great souls of our time.

The reading of poetry is a personal experience, and Welborn's poems create in me a very personal, spiritual response. For that reason I decided to collect as many of them as possible and make them accessible to others. Over the years Welborn has filled his little black notebooks with more than two thousand poems, most of which have been lost, "left behind," or given away. Many of the poems in this volume were provided by Conner Logsdon, who generously made his collection available to us. Welborn and I express our appreciation to him. We are also grateful to Mavie Farley for the hours of typing that she devoted to preparing the manuscript for publication.

Among the previously published poems in this collection, "Johnny Appleseed" first appeared in the *Ada Evening News*. The *News* provided from its files the following unpublished poems: "The Blind Singer of the Subways," "The Ferryboat," and "A Publisher's Stock Boy." The following poems first appeared in *Poetry*: "In Indian Territory," "The Squatter," "Southwestern Tornado," "A Squatter's Wife," "The Vanished River," "In Early Spring," "Moonrise After Midnight." "The Wild Children and She" first appeared in *The New Republic*. The following poems appeared in *Saturday Review*: "Killers of the Old West," "We Met Osages," "Danger," "In the Eden That Is Erie's," "The Wild Children and She," "The Oleander," "The Rose in the Book," "Roll Away, Iowa Corn," "The Rodeo Comes to Boston Garden," "The Home-Town Paper," "The Great River and Small."

Finally, and in behalf of the poet, I express sincere thanks to Stanley P. Wagner and Raymond James, Jr., whose generous help made this book possible.

GUY W. LOGSDON
Director of Libraries
University of Tulsa

Tulsa, Oklahoma
April 15, 1970

 CONTENTS

THE GREAT RIVER AND SMALL

Sleeping by the stump-fire, ashes in
His eyes, the small man rolled a little nearer
The warmth, away from dawn's malarial grin
Widening over cypress; the dull river,
Loaded from pigsties and commodes of sin,
Uncomprehending, knew not the sleeper, the bearer.

Not for the river were his snatches of sense,
The great octopus gulf-bound with its seizure
Of rich topsoil, the nation's gutlike rinse
Bearing the offal of cities in its leisure,
And abortions from those areas, safe, immense,
Where millions in its tentacles slept secure.

The sleeper by the stump-fire, chilled through and
        through,
At length arose, staggering under the burden
On his shoulders, as wild verses sucked anew
Which no man living had as yet concurred in.
Crazed with wild verses which like brain-greenery
        grew—
Out of the swamp to the tavern someone stirred in.
Hunched over beer, to himself the small man sang,

To a bar girl's puzzlement, the dizzy
Life of dumb hordes upriver, and he rang
Bells in heaven, which nobody heard.

                              Crazy,
He hit his fist on the bar with a bang:
The barmaid muttered, "Brother, take it easy."
How tell her of the huge country his shoulders bore?
He cried, "Rimbaud, Rimbaud, had I your devotion
I would surge with its song to the sea shore."
The fat slow river soundlessly in motion,
The small man sniffled, pushed his mug for more,
Dragging the whole Midwest down to the ocean.

As from a hailing horn, I still can take
Spirit of the echoes dying far:
The frontier moving in the sunset's wake.
Farther and farther the western eagles are
That soar above the lost, blind caravan,
Scouts of the stars to find the one strait gate.
If gate there is, to prove the myths of man,
There they will beat their wings, and beckon late.

Oh, I will follow; when my spirit's presses
Grow dry and dusty, with my palate burning,
The horn will sound, though loneliness distresses.
And I may see the twilight wings returning
When I at last have found their valor's vine
And then have filled a staunch skin with the wine.

The steel-nerved and magnanimous men,
Whose slaying are made legends now,
Romance wraps: they kill not again.
A special breed let us allow
Glory, for valor and the story.
Since now is born mythology,
Since now in beauty records gory
Take flight into posterity,
Leave this not out: how one man died—
Finger and trigger blown away,
His gun fell cocked on the floor at his side.
Bless the precision of that play!
The bullet-honeycombed border hell
Has vanished, but strange beauty veils
The spot forever, while the yell
Of killer's triumph never fails
To yield a sound when twilights pass
On the green mossy buffalo grass!

The fires of earth are many and diverse,
Beautiful all, and music they befriend
With warmth of soul where noble sounds rehearse,
Like Spring and love and song they leap and end;
Bugles of beauty are the redbud's fires;
In lonely eyes the fires of love are stars;
Cities and forests and the mighty lyres
Have known their awful surge like sweeping wars.

A little fire that sang itself to sleep
Made music like a master to my dreams,
Under the pines peace in the mountains' deep,
A fire of peace, a fire with tender gleams
Upon my sanguine muse of youth and love
Like a mild friend. But when I stirred with morn
Gray-cold, and piled on fagots from above—
It barked a sharp word like a thrust of thorn.

 NEWS ON THE PRAIRIES

No news was mean when men were lone
Within the wild's immensity;
But news was magnified and known
Enormous for its rarity.
From the lost world a word again
Illumined space with human hues:
To simple and ferocious men,
Sweet as a woman's breast was news.

The brutelike length of prairies swung
The weight of all their awe upon
An item on a telling tongue;
Then news had grandeur like the dawn.
Piteously, the starved soul reached,
Out of its grown-half-savage mind,
Out of the night that news impeached,
Toward the splendors of its kind.

The native-foreigner, with a quizzical look,
    Wandered our altered streets an April morn,
Hunting all eyes in haunts that he forsook
    Even before familiar eyes were born.

Young girls who sipped with straws from cups in cars
    Surveyed him from their mothers' eyes
        unknowing,
As if eyes were but heirlooms of faded stars
    Worn by the young though time's new winds
        are blowing.

Laughter in them was not for him again
    To join with comfortable convivial grace:
Worry in them was not confided pain
    His counsel or his courtesy could erase.

Not a stone, nor a path, nor a house, nor spire
    Brought back the sweet pain he had long
        foreguessed—
(This melancholy moment was an old desire)—
    Indifference in eyes was bitterest.

And he thought: Better if time could unmesh
    Unto the time I turned expatriate,
Even that hour with their darts in my flesh—
    And feel forever, as then, these eyes' hate!

This is a dulled dream, the gray town
    That settles in sleep and roses here,
Visibly, almost, sinking down
    To its mouldered pioneer.

Recall no more its rough young limbs,
    Or fiery heart from hectic birth:
It stares with dotard eye that dims
    On leaning muffled heart to earth.

Its artery no more its own,
    But taken by the distant cities,
It heeds the hurrying life alone,
    And with disdain: perhaps it pities.

With individual fragrance over,
    Its dusk descends upon no light:
The prairie, with its wailing plover,
    May remember in the night.

WILL

High in the winds of desire I hold my head.
I brag of it to you, and may I not?
For all, the damned, the saved, the live, the dead,
All men are proud of their will. My heart is hot
For courage and for excellence and grace,
As millions are—and have you seen a man
However wretched, beaten, furtive-eyed,
But who, off-guard and bragging, says "I can,"
His valor in a vestige of his pride,
With reminiscence on his face?

Call it unworthy what he calls his worth:
His strength that kept him, till the brutal toll
Of mischance, his erect and solid earth:
The ballast of a body is its soul:
Our will in what we think, and what we do,
And still may boast of even if we're bitten
By frost, broken by storm, or far misled
On darker nights than death. So I have written,
"High in the winds of desire I hold my head,
And keep my word, my Old West bond, still true."

When you escaped, your misdeed died
　　Within the generous prairie's night.
And your dishonor no more was cried—
　　You were washed clean with morning's light.

The absolution freed you like the plover
To come and go, night behind for cover.

Innocent as the born in Christ,
　　You were adjudged by grass and sky
And morning wind, wildflower-spiced;
　　The snipe at ponds you galloped by
Were unsuspecting and uncaring
　　How your forgiven soul was faring.

Thus shriven of your past and shame,
　　You went among strangers easily,
And chose you an unquestioned name,
　　Or else reserved identity.
And no man ever asked you whence you came.

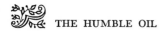

Just as he stood a century-half ago,
With folded arms, though now his figure's bent,
Upon the limestone cliff stands Choctaw Joe,
As sun creeps down the way his fathers went.

While stars in derrick-crowns light one by one,
The great field teems below him like a hive;
But where the watcher stands, a day is done,
With skies above him silently alive.

The wind falls at his feet and drops all sound
Of the world's wheels turning limitless
On plains and oceans, from the ravished ground
Beneath his gaze, and under his loneliness.

Down there are his the royalties of a King—
He has not counted them, nor cares how much;
He leaves his gold in others' measuring,
A Midas unmindful of his mark, the touch.

But like a slow rejection of the gift
His turning seems, soft-blanketed by dusk;

And mournfully he creeps behind the cliff
Along a path where no deer leaves its musk;

Where no wild turkey gobbles goodnight last
Beyond his chink-clayed cabin dark and damp;
He holds its door till in his dogs have passed,
Then lights the humble oil in his one lamp.

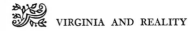 VIRGINIA AND REALITY

To every beautiful face
I've known, I've given a mind
Of my own making, to place
In my brain, image-lined.

Something you may not be,
Virginia, I've of you,
In a spacious galaxy,
Of beauty and error, too.

As of the stars I dream
That light may be behind,
More than myself you beam,
Lovely moon of my mind.

 RECLUSE

Within the cabin of my heart,
My coonskin cap hangs on the wall,
My rifle rests on antlers' prongs;
And I am snug while snowflakes fall.

With buffalo loin on the blaze,
I bend to my moccasin's repair:
In hibernation I am held
Like a bole's full-bellied bear.

An hundred miles or more away
The city and machines and men;
Here I have hidden in my hills
That love may not find me again.

The Pawnee may attack with spring,
But by his arrow I shall rest—
No more will I creep city streets
With a flint buried in my breast.

I walked a rutty road on blackjack hills,
And saw the sparse, pale corn tented on rocks
Of mean, red slopes. Beauty has no thrills,
I thought, is stunted here of all God's places.
I saw how meager were the autumn shocks—
These fields were women with less lovely faces;
But I have heard that beauty hides when hunted
In fairer spots than where her charms are stunted;

And I've these hills in trust of love and pride,
I know that otherwhere I'll not forget them;
Oh, I may go, and fate may give and take,
But for their homeliness, I'll not regret them,
Or, parvenu, find reasons to deride:
For I have ties with them time cannot break.

What would Washington Irving think
If he saw this country again today?
What Chouteau?
                Once, was a vision
On the banks of the Verdigris
That the cracked fiddles warmed at night—
There was a depth to exultation
Among those commonly conscious they
Were the sparks of a great beginning.
There was exuberance welled up
In their astonished souls, for Beauty
The Virgin, had spoken of romance
Ingenuously: their hearts were full.
Then in the morning, the renewed promise:
The river with bleached bars, the rising
Mists; the pigeons seeking gravel;
And a silence of Expectancy
In which a sound was challenged, held
For scrutiny by the startled hills
That guard the priceless lands beyond.
There was a promise then for Time
Too silently exciting to be said,
Imagination overwhelmed
By a foreknowledge which, a century done,
We find, in many sordid ways, not so.

 JOHNNY APPLESEED

(A nomad of the Great Plains from 1820 to 1840)

With appleseed to give for old love's sake,
    By every squatter's settlement
Roamed Johnny Appleseed with his heartbreak;
    Love's haunted harbinger, he went
With gentle crazy eyes through that lone land,
    Seeking the heart of Man his brother:
The seed of silver apples in one hand,
    The seed of golden in the other.

In every dale he dreamed the snowy bosoms
    Of apple trees in spring would rise,
The kiss of young love under apple blossoms
    A graven image in his eyes.
Ah, Johnny Appleseed, how delicate
    And beautiful your wild ways were,
Tramping our wilderness early and late,
    Sowing your memories of Her.

He knew a redskin loves as well as white,
    When murderous Cheyennes grew mild
To take the seed that made his soul grow light

31

And laughing as a flattered child:
A wise child might suspect and understand
    What elders studied to discover
In seed of silver apples in one hand,
    And seed of golden in the other.

Great poets wander in the world, and bleed
    For one girl lost, their sum of song,
And one of those was Johnny Appleseed,
    To whom all Creation gave a tongue
Fulfilled in Ozark or in prairie loam,
    Whenever boy and girl in bliss,
Beneath the blossom-duplicated dome
    Of starlit heaven, blend and kiss.

 OKLAHOMA DUCK FLIGHT

For beauty's seeds sprayed down by frosted wind
To sow the pond with bloom of hue at dawn,
I waited for them, waited by the shore,
Until the edges of the wind were gone
Beneath the smoothing of the sunbeam planes;
And all that day, and all that Autumn, I
Kept watch for them across the smoky sky.

That year, for once, our fields were parched and bare:
This sensing, they avoided our province,
And I thought maybe, like wild pigeons, they
Were finished; till, down where rice ripened since,
I heard they milled as usual and as many;
Then I was glad, watching the fall hills burning,
And waiting as one waits love unreturning.

So here they are, the men of blood,
Booted and spurred, from all the West!
On my lone life, need they intrude?
The broad-brimmed hat, the piebald vest,
Disturb my hard-won solitude.

High in the Boston Garden, they
Present the triumph of the Plains,
Repeat the godless, golden day,
While I sit brooding on my pains,
Who thought to thrust the West away.

I found high thoughts in Boston, fled
Boots on the boardwalk, Western whang:
Ashamed of that wild Past long-dead,
I find it flares with all its tang
In Boston Garden, overhead.

No, I never broke a horse,
Lassoed a steer, or set a brand—
I cared so little for raw force
My soul fled to this town to stand
With flesh not harsh, abrupt, or coarse.

My father was a cowboy, though,
And I recall fond tales of his
Of riding herd through gales and snow:
How can I shake those memories,
My soul is intermingled so!

Earth of my earth, I give, I break:
Deep pride floods in, with sighs and love
For what I hate; for Home I ache,
Its transposition high above
Boston, in the Garden, for my sake!

Over the canopy of cotton,
    Under the canopy of stars,
From sorrow a song begotten,
    A spirit breaks its bars.

Day has withdrawn his full auroral flood;
    A desuetude of rich declining light
Splashes the dark's rim like a streak of blood,
    Soon all will be dominion of the night.

A sudden eyelash flutter, the nebulous bat
    From purple aethers down to nadir sweeps;
The southern wind slips to his snow-white mat,
    Spreads down his docile musical length and
        sleeps.

Now furtive things disturb the dew no more,
    Now quitting murmurs quiet on the hill;
Now floats across the cotton's marble floor,
    The first note of the forlorn whippoorwill.

Oh, haunting-sweet, oh, sad suggestive sound,
    Whose intervaled stanzas rise again, again!

Not in the vale of Tempe more profound
    A song, more plummeting the depths of pain.

Strange voice, as from a haunted singer's mouth,
    Whose grief at night alone may be expressed;
Uncelebrated Philomel of our South,
    You wake the lyre of Poe within your breast.

Over the canopy of cotton,
    Under the canopy of stars,
From sorrow a song begotten,
    A spirit breaks its bars.

I do not know why I haunt Times Square
To buy the paper from back there—
Since time cut most, and I cut the rest
Of all the ties I had with the West.
My death-time tears are wept and done.
From youth and sorrow into the sun
I stepped, and I count as rather grand
My liberation from that land.

In New York leaps my fresh desire,
My spirit quickens with new fire;
I know I shall not see again
The oil fields and the seas of grain,
Where gas flares and wild redbuds vie
Garish beneath a purple sky,
And mockingbirds sing through the gale
Of sassafras on the Chisholm Trail.

Nostalgia murmurs, but it knows
I will not quit New York for those:
Though long-known print in Times Square brings
Odors and echoes of old springs;
And like a lone ghost lost in space
My paper is a dead friend's face.

39

From the top floor of a publishing house,
In at an artist's window I can peer;
I watch him paint, I see his merry spouse
Bring him inspiration, cheese, and beer.

Down in Greenwich Village, down below me there,
They have the sovereign happiness I lack:
As to the shelves a load of books I bear,
The souls of men grow heavy on my back.

I can pause—to gaze again, and turn
And enviously long to live and toil and thrive
Like the authors whose late lamplights burn
To break my back—oh, I'd create and wive.

 THE FERRYBOAT

We who are Staten Island bound
    Crowd to the ferryboat's rail;
Its engines hum in a hush profound,
    The wind falls, that was a gale;
In all the great harbor, no other sound,
    While sunset's golden banners trail.

Behind, Manhattan's towers gleam,
    Too fabulous for belief:
As if cloud-borne, those temples seem
    Drifting light as a leaf,
Like some religious painter's dream
    Of Heaven's city, past our grief.

Good-by, Manhattan, Mirage that fades,
    Good-by to you, tonight!
Ahead, deep in incipient shades,
    Our Isle shows scarce a light:
Though grim its cliffs that dark invades,
    One star above its dock shines bright.

There we shall rest, and rise once more—
    The ferryboat take anew

Toward the white dream city's shore,
    Silver in dawn's rose-blue:
And though we knew it all before,
    We'll watch the tall Mirage come true!

The express, jammed, gets under way—
The elbow jabbing ends at last.
There is a momentary stay—
To station next from station past—
Of human fury, face to face,
Pushing, hauling, squeezing, clinging,
Subsiding slowly in its place.
Then, plaintively, is heard his singing.

The blind Singer of the Subways, he
Electrifies the furious car:
The herd of vexed humanity
Hears him, as from another star.
The temporary angers fade,
The grandeur of his presence gains:
His music soothes those tempers frayed,
And heals Manhattan's aches and pains.

So royally metropolitan
He seems—not pitiful, though alone—
All find a friend in that brave man
Whose voice to all New York is known.
Imperial, his presence glows,

His fine pale face is lifted up;
A grateful stream of silver flows—
As he sings past—into his cup.

For such a personality never
Before lit up our Underground;
None there but would ride on forever
In the spell of its marvelous sound.
But there's the next stop—axles groan,
As brakes apply, with iron pain;
And with the singing angel gone,
The blind crowd's fury bursts again.

The smell of oil pervades this cedared scene,
We hear the put-put of drilling on the hill;
Pashofa, too, in pots upon the green,
Has savor: old and young will have their fill
Of hog and hominy this summer night.
Beware the deadline: never dare to cross
The line drawn in the crackling log heap's light
Until the fire is leapt. Ten tall braves toss
Dice in the firelight the other side the fire.
A praying Ethiopian gets their cash.
Tom-tom—tom-tom-tom ever rising higher,
While primitive emotions strain the leash.
There, presently, the dancing will begin.
The Medicine Man is jumping here and there.
Beware the deadline as you saunter in,
For fear of fiery herbs they pour on your hair;
Now, at the house, squaws squat upon the porch,
Women in green, women in purple, red.
The ancient open hall is lit by torch,
Inside the house, a man coughs, almost dead.
Tom-tom-tom-tom-tom-tom. Two striped poles
     stand.
A willow put between them with bright streamers;
Two watchers of the deadline, whip in hand,
Wait, as motionless as dusky dreamers. . . .

A mule-drawn wagon bearing squaw and brave
Pulls up beside their limousines parked nigh. . . .
An Indian whoop, a voice from out the grave
Of Oklahoma's past, splits wide the sky.
Tom-tom. . . . They come to drive away the evil
Spirits that darken a sick warrior's house,
With color, with dancing, feast and fortnight revel,
The evil spirits fly when redskins carouse.
All's set. "Watch 'em deadline, White Brother.
    Come,
Eat Pashofa with us, dance by drum."

In front of me, my walk, the blue sky cloaks
The bowed brown immobility of oaks.
Softness I shall seek for, with song's nets:
Calves' eyes entrance me quiet as violets.

Manure on the fields has the very smell
I should expect of a soft-ringing bell.

Gentleness I am winning of the earth,
For my mild flower, from the Springtime's birth.

The birds? I miss the birds. Up from the root
The trees will call them with a liquid lute.
You can't hear it? Ah, man, but that's our lot—
A brown-eyed setter smells what we do not.

Like a long snake, the wagon train
Wound across the lush-green plain.
Beside it, ready for alarm,
Outriders rode, rifle on arm.
Toward the sunset, it crawled on,
And flowers of the Southwest shone.
Golden rudbeckia burned afar
To brand on the plain a flaming scar;
Modest centaurea were scattered about
Among gaillardias' gleaming rout;
Pink phlox plaited the prairie's hem,
And coreopsis made a diadem.
Savage and hushed, a beautiful land,
Awaiting Catlin's marvelous hand,
Spread wide before the pioneer eyes,
Beneath the brilliant evening skies.

A sinister, bloody, lonely trail,
Where faith might tire and strength might fail,
How could it be, amid such beauty?
And yet, so worn by dusty duty,
So wracked by invisible peril near,
Perhaps little beauty saw the pioneer.

Hunt no more for swift Adventure
On these plains the grange has won;
Seed in the soil and seed in the womb
Time sowed to tame the fiery one,
Arose to catch him in confines,
But he was off like Daniel Boone,
And few men know where now to find him,
Save those, perhaps, beyond the moon.

Life is scarce worth the living without him;
Lord, to have been a young man when
He rode his roan that was Poetry.
Lord, to have been a young man then—
When he struck out into a storm—
His Horse's hooves on stones a-spark—
And rode like God behind the lightning
Of his gun's flash in the dark!

With milling and mooing at end of day,
The herd lie down with heavy thuds;
The mist-like dust has caught wild May,
And it showers like a dew from buds.

Between two hills, the hesitant star,
As on a stairway, pauses supreme;
Glowing as to the thin guitar,
And to the valley's voice of dream.

Softness beguiles tired reflexes;
The lonely beauty tunes the gruff—
And toward the Yellow Rose of Texas,
Tenderness moves the bronzed and rough.

Their voices join; for each alone,
Her features flower in the fire.
... The flinty drover, with a groan,
Stirs wryly a toddy, to retire.

The child's throat of the creek laughs out,
At some secreted comedy;
The mulberry chucks it purple pebbles—
And birds in thick green privacy
Keep a sweet conflict of fresh sound.
I would be hermit in this hour,
Claiming as mine the wild wood's length,
By every oddity of flower,
By jeweled chalcedony ledge,
By treasure-troves of beauty found,
I'd sing my heart out to the land!

Oh he knew a thrill, an unashamed
Vigorous open zest,
And with clean pride that flamed
In a pioneer's breast.

His name that the hut-huddle bore,
The first unending seed
Sown, of the simple score
At a city's core,
Was to wear many wings, indeed.

Behind him a tremendous surge,
With a ship's flotsam, beat;
He was safe on the shore,
And solid-set to shape and merge,
With honesty, into his street
Whatever the prairie's rude terrific roar
Brought in his door.

My pride of land lies in the past;
Time limns with beauty all travail,
Covers with beauty all the vast
Turbulence on the frontier trail.
Only its echoes blow back now,
And they are as faint cries that fail
Within the closure where the plow
Stubbornly plies against a gale.

The plowman in this stormy day
Plows on, an uninspiring form,
And crows pass through his skies of gray,
And speak his plight across the farm.
But beauty and spirit still surround
The boundless, honored pioneer:
The present plowman, who is bound,
Plods in reality's sere.

I am the laziest man that ever was born—
Roll away, roll away, Iowa corn!
I don't want to work or do a blessed thing
But in the Midwest twilight sit and sing
And clap my hands for joy of being born—
Roll away, roll away, Iowa corn:
Roll away, sparkling like a growing soul,
Roll away beyond the glowing knoll!
The highway's houselike fleets are roaring on,
But in the silence, after they are gone,
I lay my ear down on the throbbing ground,
And hear with all my soul a nobler sound:
Deep in America's heart I hear the drumming
Of the Grand Singing Years majestically coming—
And I clap my hands again because I was born:
Roll away, with all my cares, Iowa corn!

Tramping through a Western state, weary in spirit
The young poet felt he might not last long enough.
"God," he said, "nobody honors merit;
High my eagle flies, but I do need love."
So God, on his way to church, dropped by his bank,
Phoned, came out, carnation glowing in lapel.
He heard the vagabond's shy plea, fished in a flank,
And bestowed a quarter. He said: "Work, son,
    while you're able."

Then there she was, his dream girl in the ticket
    window:
With Theda Bara showing, he could see
The film's star on the boards, but framing a show
Of the town's blonde beauty, who lifted up a knee.
Her blue eyes fastened on him, forlorn on the curb,
She staged a show for him as customers came,
(All of whom she knew) pushed out her breasts,
    superb,
That he might see her greatness in his shame.

The flower shop was open, so he bought a rose.
She kept it in her diary—later in his book:

And of this, oftentimes she said: "Lord knows,
I knew he was a famous man—from his look."
But she didn't know, as town librarian,
When she served the book in distaste and mistrust,
To the grimy gray-haired tramp, that he was the man
Who wrote it, forty years undisturbed in its dust.

The tribes believed a river of beasts
Flowed underground eternally,
That rumbled under earth's dark breasts,
And looked out on its way to the sea.
Somewhere in the mysterious south,
An enormous mountain cave belched forth
A shaggy maelstrom from its mouth,
That spread in turbulence to the north.
No river known as thunderous
As this upon the prime of plains—
It still is too miraculous
To mock the myth, and this remains:
That never eyes were more amazed
Than those to watch its mad wave pass,
Or see its body's spread that grazed
In eddies on the blue-stemmed grass.
And I have wondered on this river's
Marvel more than I can tell:
But I would be with those believers
Of the fabled miracle,
Rather than stand without the wonder
On its imaged prairie shore,
Nor listen for the fearful thunder
Man may hear no more.

When his spirit neared outbreak,
It stormily gathered over drink;
His heavily clouding mood would make
Flashes of fire half rise and sink.
Thus seasoned citizens knew the signs
Of something like a cyclone brewing
In the southwest corner of Kline's—
At least, there would be something doing
Like sudden elemental change.
From the dark center of the storm
Came rumbles ominous and strange,
And all eyes watched the brooding form
Become, if not as conical
As menacing as a Kansas twister.
He rose—tremendous, dark, and tall—
And caught a spangled girl, and kissed her;
He whirled her like a slender tree,
And chairs and tables too went whirling.
He swept the bar down gustily,
And up the boardwalk he went swirling—
Flame-surrounded hell unpent—
As men sought shelter in a hurry
From this abrupt, magnificent
Epitome of human fury!

"How goes the West we came to win for you?
Pity our poor bones, Stranger, for we wonder
What your golden time has brought forth new.
We sleep beneath another daylong thunder
Than the herd that marked the seasons once;
What signal from the strict stars have you heard,
Oh fortunate above our failing bones,
That turns our plains to Paradise, what word
Bids men such fevered haste to hold the truth
We could not learn, whose oxen's tread was slow?
What music from the giver gives you ruth?
Heaven is with you, not with us, we know."

True, brave brother, what you hear speaks well
Of what should all be Paradise descried.
Ask me no more, for more I should not tell,
Who would look backward to the day you died.
Share with me all that memory retains
Of sights and sounds and dreams forgotten here;
Perhaps you heard a viol on the plains
A summer night when stream and skies were clear;
And you sleep safe whose heart was all aflame
In once a freedom finer than another;
Your grandeur shines through my despair and shame,
When I must muse on mendicants, proud brother.

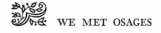

We hailed them like a ship upon the main;
The band of them rode like a stately ship
On the fluid green of the silent plain.
Since the shower, lilacs were a-drip—
Hazes like halos could have hidden sails
As they obscured the body sailing by,
And far beyond, like spray, twined volatile veils.
We called, and the call rang deep within the sky.

One rode toward us with a lifted hand,
And in that hand his feathered shafts and bow;
Dismounted from his piebald pony, and
Before our swart interpreter, a stone's throw,
Made talk, and then advanced with gallant tread,
Swinging bow and shafts. The scarlet frock,
The deerskin leggings, the eyes in his proud head
That flashed—these gave him, oh, a godlike look!

He talked, and he pointed, and he noted us;
Gave our directions through a distant gap;
Grunted at a gift, and flashed his eyes, and thus
He marched away, leggings and frock a-flap.
He leaped on his mare, and in a trice was gone
Back to his band—and then the ship moved on.

Her pastime was to wander down the stream,
The crystal stream that wound through the
     shortgrass;
After her lonely toil, to stray and dream,
And watch the plover come to drink and pass.
She knew the trees beyond would yet befriend her,
The far dear cluster that her steps would gain
Would soothe her hillborn heart at dusk, and mend
     her
Until the stars with beauty end her pain.
This was a small disloyalty she needed
To keep the courage of her love aloft;
If she felt shame when in the hush she heeded
The sounds where pain-racked on his cot he coughed,
Little she knew her heroism in doing
The harsh work of the sick man's desperate lot.
So, as he coughed, she hummed a tune, renewing
Romance in times that she had not forgot,
And sought the kindly trees to keep her whole,
As in the hills of her nativity:
Lest the prairie overwhelm her alien soul,
And hurl upon her swift insanity.

After New York, he stood once more
　　In the long wideness of the street
That knew him well those years before,
　　But as strange now as his old defeat.

This was the West where he was born
　　In a day when the Old undimmed
Blazed its sunset last in scorn
　　On the New, arriving tame and trimmed.

Here Geronimo and captors came,
　　The old chief unbroken but unfanged;
Here once, in sunset's failing flame,
　　The horse barn where four men were hanged;

And gone the redbrick bank grown gray,
　　The new one's marble in its stead;
Nor those his friends of that far day,
　　Though some had faces of the dead.

So he walked on, with his father's face
　　Perhaps—or most his fearful mother's—

And stopped before a fallen place
    And her hydrangeas, now another's.

No anxious voice to welcome him:
    Too far, too many city bars
Since first he tried, when faith was dim,
    To walk on stilts toward the stars.

 DANGER

Upon wild plains omnipotent,
A conquering quality Danger was.
You saw it always imminent,
A sly shadow on the grass.

It was an agent in the air
Active as sunshine, yielding health
And Death, but not Death everywhere.
An able antitoxin for fear,
A forthright courage it fostered by stealth.

Sometimes it grew bold, and you saw
Danger formidable of form,
A demon, lightning on the draw.
Likely you never lived to speak of harm.

But it would kill, as it could cure,
By stealth. A banjo banishing care,
A circle in the campfire's light,
A wriggling figure in the night,
A lively music on the wind,
A screaming arrow, and an end.

It was a presence you endured
And hated—but it had discipline.
It hovered until you were inured
And finally purged of fear within.

Then you perceived its purity
And you sought it as a lover seeks virginity.

THE WILD CHILDREN AND SHE

(For a Boston girl who taught among the Chickasaw
Indians in 1857)

Now they are running with the wind,
    The wild children and she;
For they have put away books from mind,
    And follow home a honeybee;
She has forgotten her far off kind,
    They have found the honey tree.

It is twilight; under the tree, dark;
    They are fed on golden food;
They lie on warm grass beneath the arc
    Of heaven's sound-lit solitude:
And she tends now the musical spark
    Human in her brown brood.

Lonesome, becoming lonesomer,
    The wild children and she;
What if an old love ache in her
    As she murmurs poetry?
Soft are the poet's words that stir
    The wild hearts at her knee.

The wise owls wake before the dawn,
    The tired stars shake when they hear;
Swift the wild children and she are gone
    In the change and chill of air;
Where they have risen, day will shine on
    Dewy wild deer bells there.

Geronimo, imprisoned, dreamed
    His end was all for this?—
Or renegade braves with bandits schemed,
    For you and me to kiss?

Strange I should think of those, my dear,
    As fox grapes on the vine
Make arbor for us reigning here,
    While sumac glows to wine.

Swans that breast the ravine,
    As if reflected from
The blue above the green,
    The shining dogwoods come.

As we ride faster now,
    Swift redbuds flash in briar,
As from a holy bough—
    Sprays of the heaven's fire.

 AUTUMN LOVE

Now the plover cry at night,
    Soon will cry the geese—
Shadows in the pale moon's light
    That flicker in her fleece.

So at midnight I go walking
    Abroad, to hear again
The great gray skies with mystic talking
    To the town and plain.

What connection their talk has
    With my young love and me,
She'll not know, nor that I pass
    Her place, for she'll not see.

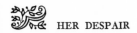 HER DESPAIR

A shy despair upon her beauty lives,
A delicate lovely thing is her despair;
Soft like her skin must be the thought that gives
The beautiful gloom her gentle features bear.
Happiness would break the clear design
Of purest pain upon this finest face,
The sensitive imprint with no bitten line
Of knowledge on her shadow of dark grace.
Calm in presentiment, the nerves of night
Throb in her as gay blossoms throb with sun,
With nought of fear in her clean eyes' clear light,
The velvet-souled, the shadow-friendly one.
And all hardbitten ones whom beauty hurts
When light and heedless, having had their hour,
Love her, for beauty reaps its deep deserts
When Sorrow sees its heartbreak in full flower!

In the Eden that is Erie's
I came on a sudden sunburst of cherries.
Tramping along the lakeshore road,
I might have been Adam, since it was Eve
Whose cherry cheeks of sunset showed.
Forbidden fruit, I did believe,
Were millions and millions of reddest gems,
Spilled, glistening rubies on stems.

Nobody knows how many I stole,
And God knows if I've saved my soul,
But there my Paradise I gained,
Dusty, penniless, alone;
Tramping along the lakeshore road,
My shirt front with wine of cherries stained.
I walked with secret riches all my own,
Nobody hated and nobody owed—
And my pockets full of stolen cherries
In the Eden that is Erie's!

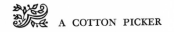

Though she was skin and bones, the fields were white;
She must gather to the edges of the night,
Then call the cows, and listen for a bell
As if it were the last sound possible
From ending chores she feared to have end so.
Inevitable loneliness when day would go—
The wall that she could push away no more
Would close around her, take roof, shut the door,
A darker house within the kind of house
Where most would never once have dared to drowse
Alone. But she would clutch at one boll yet,
And straighten aching bones to mop the sweat,
And struggle with the sack to make a stir
On to the drooping stalk ahead of her;
So, finally, release her shoulders, rise
Tasting the bitter dusk with mouth and eyes,
To go like age, calling across the sloughs,
A call like pleading for other than the cows—
Go into the house, and there a vigil keep,
More mournful than the whippoorwill, to weep
After one look down the road beneath the moon
For three tall sons that went away in June.

My mother played Chopin, the time it bloomed
That summer outside her window, in a tub
She watered every day though it was doomed.
Wind raged, dust sifted, and she rose to rub
Piano, mantel, sills with a rag.

                    I remember
Her face (glimpsed in this window of my years)
With her fingers on the keys, when her oleander
Bloomed in a last euphoria, her tears
Not for the failing tree, but my father's crisis
In his bank—while the drouth-bit country crushed
All but her will to shut out those gravelly voices
Everywhere flying as wind and rumors rushed.
Then one day, while still the sprays kept green our
      lawn,
My father came home, forgot his favorite cigar,
And stood at her window with something in him
      gone—
A dead oleander fixed in his sick stare.
He tiptoed out, and dragged the prisoned wilt
Quietly to the rear.

                But where the tub had been,
A death-pale ring of yellow like his guilt
Outgleamed the glistening lawn's bright bluegrass
      green.

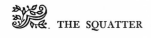

You were a squatter, a young man
Alone with one.
You had plowed a pitiful plot,
And day was done.
You watched a multitude of pigeons
Eclipse the sun.

Wild turkeys gobbled in the thicket,
Tame ones in your yard.
Your well sheave with its sudden shriek
Contentment scarred.
You stared upon the plot you'd plowed,
And life seemed hard.

Then the prairie, armed with terror
Of its solitude,
The mighty prairie arose around you,
Startled you stood,
While imagined whoops of fiends
Congealed your blood.

Gently, a hand crept into yours,
Come from behind—

A blest support and firm. The prairie
Sank, resigned,
Docile again; and terror faded
That love faced blind.

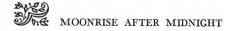

This is the alien ethereal hour
Positive neither of day nor night,
When dew is a timid attenuated shower
Slipping with shy step through haze's white.

How intimate the Moon is, she being
Far from the glory-jealous Sun!
Delightfully truant is her fleeing
Fast up the sky till her heights are won.

The Sun denied the birds to sing,
Long ago the Sun denied their race
To sing till dawn's cocksure of wing
Above his song-accepting face.

Day's cheaters were the birds at night,
If they were awake. Their secret keep.
Such music in this tender light
From hidden ones who dream in their sleep!

Aunt Martha shunned the world at eighty-two
　　For a contemplative year;
Of hell and heaven, only this she knew:
　　Her loved ones still were here;
And in one plot of ground, they yet were true,
　　Awaiting her whom they held dear.

Safe from God and safe from Satan, she
　　In that enclosure knelt each day;
She raised the forms of youth in memory,
　　As she knew them, shining, gay,
And when they ringed around her, silently,
　　She heard what roses have to say.

The roses, nodding, spoke that language pure,
　　Which Earth speaks, meaning to her, Soon.
The only speech of which she could be sure:
　　Here, shut from sun and moon,
No demons or archangels to endure,
　　Were those with whom she would commune.

No purgatorial prayer to the Power
　　For Heaven's glorious utmost bliss:

But to the Earth that bore the grave-fed flower
    She leaned old lips to kiss:
From dewy sun-up to the twilight hour,
    She gave her hoarded love to this.

To melt into the murmuring mould of love
    Down under, where her scented dream
Anticipated no winged Life above:
    For evening's silver gleam
From God's high family-table did not move
    Her clutching heart, close to Death and them.

Perhaps she was right. Within the grave inwrought
    There may be some gay ghost-life there.
It could turn out more than her strange dream
    sought,
    With music in that under-air.
For grave-clothes cling, as Rilke gravely taught,
    To walkers not upon the Holy Stair.